BIBLE MIRACLES

32 DAILY DEVOTIONS AND JOURNAL TO INSPIRE *TODAY'S WOMAN*

BARBARA SURRATT HEMMING

Xulon
PRESS

Copyright © 2010 by Barbara Surratt Hemming

Bible Miracles: 32 Daily Devotions and Journal to Inspire Today's Woman
by Barbara Surratt Hemming

Printed in the United States of America

ISBN 9781609571306

All rights reserved solely by the author. The author guarantees all contents are original and do not infringe upon the legal rights of any other person or work. No part of this book may be reproduced in any form without the permission of the author. The views expressed in this book are not necessarily those of the publisher.

Unless otherwise indicated, Bible quotations are taken from The King James Bible.

www.xulonpress.com

TABLE OF CONTENTS

ACKNOWLEDGEMENTS vii
INTRODUCTION ix
THE MIRACLE OF THE BIBLE 13
THE CREATION 20
THE POWER OF THE CROSS 24
AN ATTITUDE OF WORSHIP 30
DRAWING A LINE 35
THE MASTER'S TOUCH 40
WORDS OF LIFE.................................. 47
DESPERATE FAITH 51
DINGS, DENTS AND A FLOATING
    AXE HEAD 56
TAKE THEM TO JESUS 62
DO THE SIMPLE THING 68
REMOVE THE SCALES........................ 73
NEGATIVE WORK ENVIRONMENT....... 79
UNSEEN HELPERS............................. 85
HELPING TO HEAL THE EARTH 90
LOOK BEYOND MERE SIGHT.............. 95
USE WHAT YOU HAVE 102

STORMY WEATHER	107
IT'S ALL ABOUT OBEDIENCE	114
MIRACULOUS LANDING	119
A DREAM DEFERRED OR GOD'S TIMING?	125
KILLER LIGHTS	130
KEEP STEPPING	136
GOD'S PLANS FOR OUR LIVES	146
LESSONS FROM THE BED	151
THE WORLD WAS NOT WORTHY	159
BIG, BOLD PRAYERS	163
WHAT'S NEXT?	168
FORMED ACCORDING TO HIS PURPOSES	174
WISDOM IN THE MIDST OF CHAOS	179
DON'T OVERLOOK YOUR BLESSINGS	183
GIVE GOD YOUR FEARS	191
END NOTES	197
AUTHOR'S NOTE TO READERS	199

ACKNOWLEDGEMENTS

This book would not have been possible without the support, prayers and encouragement of the following:

God, who called me to write and who is more than enough.

Carrie Nell, Terry, and Tony who always believed in me.

Members of my review circle (Therese Hemming, Patricia Beasley, Jenny Tomita, and Mary Ann Dentu) who provided valuable support, prayers and editorial comments that helped make this a better book.

Barbara Berschler, who provided wise counsel and legal support.

INTRODUCTION

In the gritty world of the 21st century, we're surrounded on all sides with stories of unimaginable cruelty and sadness. Living in the midst of so much turmoil, from 24-hour "bad-news" stations, to horrific instances of destruction, to threats of financial ruin, we feel helpless and uninspired to make any significant changes in our world. Is there any wonder, then, that our relationships, careers, and health suffer as we try to tackle these situations on our own?

Women, in particular, lead such hectic lives. We play multiple and pivotal roles in the lives of those around us. We are wives, daughters, mothers, sisters and aunts. We are friends and caretakers of family members and others. We work inside the home and outside the home, and all places in between: as factory and office workers; soldiers, firefighters, and police officers; and entrepreneurs. We are stay-at-home moms, single mothers, homeschooling moms, students, and volunteers. At one time or another, we may have filled many of those roles simultaneously. Name any occupation or worthwhile endeavor and chances are women are not only actively involved, but are also helping to lead the effort. Whether at home, in the marketplace, or volunteering in the church or community, the stress of our day-to-day routines can leave us feeling drained, empty, and seemingly without hope. Above all, we need to be inspired and encouraged.

Few things can inspire and generate more hope than the Bible and the miracles it contains. The Scriptures have brought comfort and peace to millions during times of crisis and despair. They provided hope and encouragement to me as I raised my children alone. And they are still teaching and inspiring trust in the Savior of mankind. With inspiration from above, we can draw closer to Jesus, knowing the present situation is not beyond His power and grace to help.

It's my desire that the devotions contained in this book help draw you closer to mankind's only true confidence and inspiration, Jesus Christ. My prayer is that you be inspired anew through the process of reading through these Scriptures and devotions, and journaling specific insights the Holy Spirit gives you. As you reflect on the character and power of God shown in these Bible miracles, and through the lives of ordinary men and women today in similar circumstances, know that you can find the solutions to your problems in Jesus Christ.

Come. Join me as we journey through these miracles from the Bible. May they inspire you, as they inspire me, to move deeper into the heart of God.

THE MIRACLE OF THE BIBLE

For the prophecy came not in old time by the will of man: but holy men of God spake as they were moved by the Holy Ghost. (2 Peter 1:21, KJV)

Read 2 Peter 1:16-21

The Bible itself is a miracle. Everything to do with the Bible is a miracle. Its very creation and existence is a miracle. It is divine in origin, written by a holy God through his human instruments. That it has survived accurately down through the ages, through oral and finally in written form, is miraculous indeed.

There is no human or Satanic attack that can destroy it. Countless attacks have been directed toward the Bible. "But the Word of the Lord endureth forever." (1 Peter 1:25, KJV)

The Bible endures despite all threats to its existence, including: [1]

- The torture and killing of many of the scholars who translated it from the original languages into modern languages.
- The murder of untold numbers of people who only wanted to read the Bible in their native languages.

- Public burnings of the Bible throughout the centuries.
- The persecution and martyrdom of ordinary individuals who merely had a Bible in their possession.
- The ridicule and false accusations today by many about the content and validity of the Bible.

In spite of these and many more attacks, the Bible not only survives intact, but flourishes. The Bible has remained as America's favorite book across all societal groups. [2]

As the divinely inspired Word of God, the Bible tells about God's love and care for us and His plan to save mankind from the penalty of sin. It records miracles that occurred to the people mentioned within its pages. It informs us how a holy God expects mankind to approach him and how He deals with humankind. Were it not for the accuracy of the events it records, and the detail of those events, the legitimacy of the Bible would have fallen apart after so many centuries of questions, speculations, and persecutions. But the Bible endures.

It has influenced for the good the move of entire nations and civilizations, inspired poets, artists, lawmakers, statesmen, Presidents, kings and queens, individuals, religions, charities, and countless other endeavors. Because of its divine and lasting influence for good, millions still turn to the Bible daily as the unfailing and true Word of God for daily living. They seek the comfort, inspiration, and wisdom it offers. Its power to change lives and touch the hearts of men and women and rid them of a lifetime of destructive habits is renown. It is blessed by countless unnamed others who draw sustenance from its contents. No one can explain how this is done except by the miracle-working power of God and His Word.

Scripture itself points to the enduring power of the Word. Isaiah 40:8 says, "The grass withereth and the flowers fadeth: but the word of God shall stand forever." (KJV) With such powerful help easily within our reach, is there any wonder we return to the Bible time and time again for the hope and solutions it offers?

JOURNAL THE ISSUE:

1. Briefly tell below what the Bible means to you.

---

2. Do you have a regular time of Bible reading outside church? If not, can you commit to a time of regular Bible reading? To help you get started, many Bibles contain a one-year reading plan that can be used to help establish a consistent reading pattern. Or you may just start reading. If you are not familiar with the Bible, you might want to begin reading the Gospel of John in the New Testament or the Psalms of the Old Testament.

PRAYER:

Heavenly Father, help me to become more consistent in reading Your Word and not neglect it. As I continue my journey to read the Bible, help me to hear You speaking clearly through Your written Word. In Jesus' name, I pray. Amen.

THE CREATION

In the beginning God created the heavens and the earth. (Genesis 1:1, KJV)

Read Genesis 1:1-31

These first verses of the Bible startle with their clarity and brilliant simplicity. They are so simple even a child can understand them. Yet, beneath the simple language is a complexity that millions have grappled with since time began. Who is God? Why did God create the universe? What does it mean to us?

We can never fully answer these questions with our limited minds. However, we can know all we need to know based on what the whole Bible tells us. In today's passage and elsewhere, the Bible tells us that God is the Creator and Sustainer of everything (Colossians 1:17). Wherever we look, we see the majesty and power of God displayed through the miracle of His creation. Startling images of space from the Hubble telescope reveal a fraction of an immense universe. Mysterious plants and animals in our tropical forests seem to promise cures for many diseases. In addition, scientists say we may be able to extract antibodies from certain microbes that live in the ocean. The far reaches of space, the earth itself, and the depths of the seas merely hint at the miraculous creative powers of God. What a wonder God has created!

Why did God create such a vast and unique universe? The Bible says He did it for the sheer joy of it! (Revelation 4:11) The Bible says God created the universe and us for Himself, for His pleasure. We were created to reflect God's glory and holiness. What does this mean to us? Knowing a loving God created us for Himself helps us live for Him. One day, He will return to gather His own to the place He has prepared with Him. The miraculous creation that we're all a part of now is but a whisper of something in the future that is far greater.

JOURNAL THE ISSUE:

Note below your insights from the Holy Spirit concerning today's Scripture reading.

_____

_____

PRAYER:

Heavenly Father, what a marvelous thing Your creation is! I never cease to be astounded at the way You've provided everything to sustain life on the earth—both spiritually and physically. With that in mind, help me to rededicate my life to You and to caring for Your creation. In Jesus' name. Amen.

THE POWER OF THE CROSS

And Peter said unto him, Aeneas, Jesus Christ maketh thee whole: arise, and make thy bed. And he arose immediately. And all that dwelt at Lydda and Saron saw him, and turned to the Lord. (Acts 9:34-35, KJV)

Read Acts 9:32-35

As a child, most of my church attendance was with my Great Auntie. She was a devoted Christian. Her church had regular days of revival where they would invite a minister from another church to preach for a few days. To prepare, the congregation spent days in prayer, petitioning God for revival. When the visiting minister arrived and revival services got into full swing, a number of people would weep openly and testify of what God had done in their lives. As a child, this was all very mysterious to me.

That experience is small compared to the events in today's reading. But, wouldn't you have loved to have been there when Peter healed Aeneas? When Peter healed Aeneas, the people of Lydda and Saron saw it and turned to God. (Acts 9:35) Now, that's revival! And that's the power of the cross of Jesus Christ to change us from within!

Imagine the uproar that would occur if all the people who lived in two modern-day towns in America repented and turned to the Lord! The revivals that took place in 1859 and 1906 can give us an idea of how people would react to such events. Those two revivals began in America and sparked worldwide revivals. Thousands of people gave their lives to the Lord and were healed.

Because of the 1859 revival, in some New England towns, reports are that every adult there had been saved![3] What a testament to the power of the gospel of Jesus.

We may not be able to impact an entire town, but through God's grace we can have a positive effect for Jesus on those around us. We can pray for the Lord to usher in revival in our families and associates, churches, and nation. We can pray for revival to begin in our own hearts as we give ourselves more and more to Jesus. And we can look forward to seeing how the Lord does amazing things in our lives and in the lives of those around us.

JOURNAL THE ISSUE:

1. In prayer, ask the Lord to renew the fire for Him in your own heart and to help you become a woman of greater influence for Him in the lives of others.

_____

_____

2. Note below what the Holy Spirit says to you.

_____

_____

PRAYER:

Heavenly father, draw me to a quiet place where I can hear Your voice clearly. Revive my passion for you, O God. And through Your Spirit, let my love and passion for You be the forces that spur me on to spread Your love. In Jesus' name, I pray. Amen.

AN ATTITUDE OF WORSHIP

He said unto them, Give place: for the maid is not dead, but sleepeth. And they laughed him to scorn. But when the people were put forth, he went in, and took her by the hand, and the maid arose. (Matthew 9:24-25, KJV)

Read Matthew 9:18-19 and 23-26

From the moment this event opens to its end, the story of Jesus healing Jarius' daughter is saturated with astounding faith statements and actions.

Although the child was so bad off she was probably already dead, Jarius was convinced that Jesus could help. He had enough faith to ask Jesus to lay His hand on her so she would live. Even before that, he showed a wonderful attitude of worship. Verse 18 says, "he worshipped him" before saying a word to Jesus.

That was the same attitude of a longtime friend. When she told me she was undergoing chemotherapy, my heart broke for her. I wanted to run to her immediately, put my arms around her and try to comfort her. But, what she said later had me shaking my head in amazement. Rather than lamenting her illness, she said the first thing she did when she found out was to thank God for keeping her in health for all her life and began to worship Him. "Like Job," I thought. And like Jarius in today's reading.

That's how we should approach God when we pray—with a heart attitude of worship before we bring our requests to him. Sometimes, we're guilty of being so focused on our immediate troubles that we forget the good things we have in Jesus Christ. Thanksgiving seems to take a backseat to our own requests. We may rattle off a bunch of prayer requests and quickly end with, "In Jesus' name, Amen." I know that can be true of me at times. If I'm not careful, I can get a case of the "gimmies" (Gimmie this and that). Perhaps it's true of you also. During those times, we don't come to the Lord in a spirit of worship. We don't take the time to acknowledge God as the Creator of all things, the Holy One, the King of Kings, the Everlasting Father, Redeemer, the One in Whom we have our being, Savior, Wonderful, the Lord God Almighty, the only wise God, the Alpha and Omega, the Great I Am, and much more!

But, I'm learning that when we fail to acknowledge God for who He is and look only at what He does for us, we put ourselves and our priorities first—in front of God and His purposes. At the same time, we may deny ourselves the privilege of knowing His guidance and counsel. We may even miss the privilege of participating in His plan.

One way we can counter this is to remember the components of the Lord's

Prayer: worship and acknowledge God as Lord of all, ask forgiveness for our sins, and thank God for deliverance from evil. These simple things can remind us of where our priorities should lie.

JOURNAL THE ISSUE:

In the space below or on a separate sheet, write down your own prayer for yourself or a loved one using the components of the Lord's Prayer.

_____

_____

PRAYER:

Pray the prayer you've just written to God.

DRAWING A LINE

Prove thy servants, I beseech thee, ten days; and let them give us pulse to eat, and water to drink. Then let our countenances be looked upon before thee, and the countenance of the children that eat of the portion of the king's meat: and as thou seest, deal with thy servants. (Daniel 1:12-13, KJV)

Read Daniel 1:12-21

When I became a Christian, I didn't know any other Christians and didn't have a church. I longed to talk to someone about the Lord and my eye-popping discoveries in the Bible. I couldn't talk to my friends. They weren't interested in the Bible and wanted nothing to do with God. Over time, I found our relationships more and more unsatisfactory. The last straw for me came when, seated with a group of friends, I blurted out, "I believe Jesus is the Son of God."

Everyone looked at me with horror, their mouths hanging open. A few of them snickered. I was such a new believer that I didn't know what else to say, so I merely took a few sips of coffee to cover up my silence.

My efforts might have looked feeble to someone else, but they were huge for me and signaled a turnabout in my way of thinking. I had drawn a line between my friends and me that marked my growing commitment to God. Eventually, I stopped going out with them and spent my time in prayer and praise to God.

In a much more profound way, Daniel and his friends had also drawn a line between themselves and their Babylonian captors. When it could have cost them their lives, they took a bold stand for the Lord. They refused to eat the King's food that had been sacrificed to idols, a practice that was strictly forbidden by Jewish law. They relied upon God to sustain them on a diet of beans and water only. And God honored their commitment to Him.

JOURNAL THE ISSUE:

1. Maybe you too have had to take a stand for Your faith in God. No matter how small it was, note it below.

_____

_____

2. What did you learn from that time? Would you do anything differently today?

_____

_____

PRAYER:

Heavenly Father, help me to have the same kind of courage and commitment to You as the young Hebrew captives had. They drew firm boundaries marking their commitment to You. Please send Your spirit to strengthen me. Even though I may be tempted to hide my faith from others, strengthen me so that I stand as boldly as Daniel did for you. I ask this in Jesus' name. Amen.

THE MASTER'S TOUCH

Then Jesus put forth his hand and touched him, saying, "I will, be thou clean. (Matthew 8:3, KJV)

Read Matthew 8:1-4

We don't think much of our five basic senses (sight, hearing, touch, smell, taste), unless we lose one of them. The sense of touch can comfort when we're hurting and convey compassion when we're misunderstood. The positive and transforming effects of the human touch can also signify hope. So hungry are we for the touch of another human being that we've developed social rituals involving touch as a form of greeting: we shake hands, kiss, give each other a "high-five," or embrace. With each touch, we respond even more.

Medical science recognizes the nurturing power of the physician's handshake or the comfort of a light touch on the arm. A recent newspaper article pointed out that the vast majority of patients surveyed stated they liked the idea of shaking hands with their physicians. A handshake from a physician can be a forceful first step toward recovery, generating understanding and hope.

Is there any wonder, then, that a man with leprosy would respond to someone who touched him? During Jesus' time, leprosy was so feared that no one dared be anywhere near a leper, much less actually touch one. The leprous man had faith to believe Jesus could heal, but the question in his mind was *would* Jesus heal him? "Lord, if thou wilt, thou canst make me clean." (Matthew 8:2, KJV)

Jesus could have healed the man simply by His word. Instead, He chose to touch him. Jesus was willing to heal him, and the touch of Almighty God immediately drove all uncleanness and disease from the man.

Jesus is the same yesterday, today, and forever. Because the sinless blood of Jesus was shed on Calvary, His heavenly touch is still driving out sickness and the uncleanness of sin. Believe in Jesus' power to heal diseased circumstances in your life! Nothing is too hard for His loving touch.

JOURNAL THE ISSUE:

1. When we need healing in some area of the body, we should see our doctor but we should also ask Jesus for healing. That's what we learn in Matthew 7:7. Allow the powerful Scriptures that follow to minister to your spirit. Try to memorize a few of them.

   a. *Surely he hath borne our griefs, and carried our sorrows: yet we did esteem him stricken, smitten of God, and afflicted. But he was wounded for our transgressions, he was bruised for our iniquities: the chastisement of our peace was upon him; and with his stripes we are healed. (Isaiah 53:4-5, KJV)*

b. *When the even was come, they brought unto him many that were possessed with devils: and he cast out the spirits with his word, and healed all that were sick: That it might be fulfilled which was spoken by Esaias the prophet, saying, Himself took our infirmities, and bare our sicknesses. (Matthew 8:16-17, KJV)*

c. *Beloved, I wish above all things that thou mayest prosper and be in health, even as thy soul prospereth. (3 John 1:2, KJV)*

2. Lift the spirits of a sick friend or relative by mailing a few of these health-affirming Scriptures in a get-well card. Or take them when you go for a visit.

_____

_____

3. God is the healer and He knows the exact areas of our lives that need physical or emotional healing. Note below what the Lord speaks in your heart about the situation.

_____

_____

PRAYER:

Heavenly Father, I praise You that You are aware of every fevered brow and every emotional hurt we suffer. I know that we don't suffer alone; Jesus suffers with us. I ask You, Jesus, to lay Your hand on those who are in pain and need Your comfort. In Your name, I pray. Amen.

WORDS OF LIFE

And the word of the LORD came unto Jonah the second time, saying, Arise, go unto Nineveh, that great city, and preach unto it the preaching that I bid thee. (Jonah 3:1-2, KJV)

Read Jonah 3

A woman I'll call Rachael didn't think much of her supervisor. She found his management style somewhat off-putting. Their relationship was a bit tense and she tried to avoid any contact with him.

Her heart had grown cold toward him. One day, she overheard him telling another worker that he thought he was going to be fired. Despite her feelings for him, Rachael was surprised to find herself including him in her prayers.

For days, she mulled over what she should say to him, for she sensed the Lord wanted her to reach out to him. Gathering her nerve, she decided to write a note of encouragement. In the note, she told him she was sorry for his difficulties and that she was praying for him. She told him God loved him and asked him to trust Jesus to work things out for his eventual good. She left the note on his desk.

Later, he called her into his office. With a voice that was emotional and beginning to crack, he thanked her for the note and prayers and told her how much they meant to him. His sincerity touched her deeply. Through his gruff exterior, she could see how much he was hurting, and she continued to pray for him. He left the job shortly afterward, but she still remembers how little effort it can take to tell someone of the love of Jesus. We'll never know how the Holy Spirit will use our words in someone else's heart.

JOURNAL THE ISSUE:

What would you have done if you had been in Rachael's situation?

_____

_____

PRAYER:

Heavenly Father, as a believer, I have the words of life that others long to hear. Please grant me the boldness to speak a word about You to those You put in my path. I ask this in the name of Jesus. Amen.

DESPERATE FAITH

And he said unto her, Daughter, thy faith hath made thee whole; go in peace, and be whole of thy plague. (Mark 5:34, KJV)

Read Mark 5:25-34

A woman was expecting a child but early on discovered she had been exposed to a virus. The virus had the potential to wreck havoc on her unborn child's health. With the doctor holding out only faint hope and nowhere else to turn, she cried out her fears and begged God to heal her unborn child. For many months, she cried and pleaded for healing. Months later, resigned to the belief that her child would be born with serious birth defects, she found her prayers were changing. Whereas before, she was simply praying for a healthy child, now she was asking God to provide her with whatever she would need to cope with the situation because only He knew what she'd need. Then one night, she awoke with a strange sensation in her body, as if something within her body were changing. She couldn't explain how she knew but she just knew that her unborn child had been healed at that very moment.

It may be that nothing like that has ever happened to you. But you may have a friend or family member who is suffering from a serious physical condition. The doctors don't hold out much hope. Whatever the situation, you're desperate. You feel you're at the end of your rope. And you know that if there is going to be any change, now is the time for it to happen.

The woman in today's Scripture reading was determined to make contact with Jesus. She knew that Jesus had the power of God to heal her. Like this woman, you can make contact with Jesus through prayer and believe His word for what He says He will do on your behalf or that of your loved one. Today, we look to the power of Jesus' shed blood on the cross for our deliverance. We trust in His mercy toward us.

Neither of these women was satisfied with the routine answers they received. They knew inwardly there had to be another way and they kept pressing until they found it. One woman found the Messiah Himself, touched His hem, and instantly received her healing. The other kept knocking at the doors of heaven through prayer and God healed her child.

Have faith in God! You might have given up hope and think God has abandoned you, when actually this may be the perfect time for Jesus to intervene. Jesus promised that if we call on Him, He would not leave us helpless. Because of His finished work on the cross, we can ask Jesus to come to our aid. We trust in His mercy for He is the rock on which we hope.

JOURNAL THE ISSUE:

Record here what you are believing the Lord for today.

_____

_____

PRAYER:

Heavenly Father, I praise you, give You glory, and lift Your name on high. I ask that You touch me in Your mercy and grace, for You are my rock, my hope, my help, and the lifter of my head. In Jesus' name, I ask. Amen.

DINGS, DENTS, AND A FLOATING AXE HEAD

...and the iron did swim. (2 Kings 6:6c, KJV)

Read 2 Kings 6:1-7

Suppose a friend borrowed an item—something that was precious to you—and when they returned it, it was broken. Or, perhaps you've been on the opposite side. Let's say you damaged a valuable object that belonged to a friend. Suppose it was something your friend needed for their livelihood, like a car or computer? How would you feel?

In a way, the men following Elisha were in a similar situation. They told him that the place where they all lived together was too small. They borrowed an axe to build larger quarters near the Jordan River. In their quest to get the job done, the axe head separated from its handle and fell into the Jordan River. What would they say to the owner? How could they possibly repay him?

Sometimes life is like that. Without warning and by accident, the item we borrowed can break or be destroyed. But, sometimes these things happen due to our own carelessness with someone else's property. I hate to admit it, but I've often jumped out of my car without regard to the car parked next to me. I've probably left more than my share of "dings" and scratches on someone else's car, without giving it a second thought. Until I was challenged in a grocery store parking lot. Anxious to finish my to-do list, I flung my car door open. Instead of stopping, my door kept moving until the car next to me stopped it. Without missing a beat, I started to dash across the parking lot, unmindful of what had just happened. The owner, who had been sitting in his car the entire time, opened his door and protested. He began yelling at me about how I had banged up his car. Startled, I couldn't believe he was talking to me. Upon close inspection, my car door had dented his car. That's when

I realized that I had never shown regard for the cars parked next to me – it was a long-standing pattern of mine. I recognized how right he was. It was my fault and I felt ashamed. But, how do you convey this to someone who is vein-popping angry? The more I apologized, the angrier he became. When I offered to fix the door, his anger seemed to fizzle and he said no.

Days later, I still felt the sting of his sharp words. I was sorry for the damage I had caused, no matter how insignificant it might seem to some. More than that, I was dismayed at the selfishness that was in my own heart. In my haste to complete my agenda, I had not given a single thought to his property that was in such close proximity to mine. And to make matters worse,

I realized this wasn't an isolated event. Over time, it had become a terrible habit.

The Bible teaches that we should not only be concerned with our own things but also with the affairs of others. God worked a mighty miracle through Elisha that allowed him and his men to retrieve the tool and return it to its owner. He showed that, through Elisha, He had the power to take care of their every need. In a much smaller way, He used an angry driver to open my eyes to my own selfishness and lack of love.

JOURNAL THE ISSUE:

Have you ever been careless with someone else's property? Do you need to make amends? Note below what you believe the Lord is telling you about this.

_____

_____

PRAYER:

Lord, I don't want my schedule to dictate how I relate to others. Help me to slow down so I can glimpse the wondrous (and sometimes painful) ways you teach the lessons I need to learn. In Jesus' name, I pray.

TAKE THEM TO JESUS

But that ye may know that the Son of man hath power on earth to forgive sins, (he saith to the sick of the palsy,) I say unto thee, Arise, and take up thy bed, and go thy way into thine house. And immediately he arose, took up the bed, and went forth before them all.... (Mark 2:10-12, KJV)

Read Mark 2:10-12

The story of Jesus healing the paralyzed man in the above passage is a powerful demonstration of Jesus' caring, compassion, and great healing power. But it's also a powerful display of the attitude of the man's friends. The Bible says his friends brought him to Jesus to be healed. They <u>expected</u> Jesus to heal him. No doubt they had seen Jesus heal others; perhaps He had even healed members of their own families. We don't know. But, their faith was sky-high. They were convinced, beyond any doubt, that Jesus would heal their friend. The problem was getting the man to Jesus.

The man's friends had fought through the crowd and defied the Pharisees so they could get their friend to Jesus. They were determined and persistent. Picture the look on every face as they watched a man being lowered down through the roof to

Jesus! And Jesus used that incident for a great teaching moment.

That's how we should be. We should be so full of faith in Jesus' finished work on the cross that we let nothing stop us from getting to him—not our friends, families or schedules. Not even our own doubts and fears.

That's the kind of faith Jesus calls us to. It's the kind of faith that can open the door to unimagined blessings. We can have faith for the Lord to work in our own lives, but we also need the kind of faith these men had that God will work in the lives of others. Like this man's friends, we can express our faith in God in both visible and spiritual ways. The paralyzed man's friends didn't just pray for his healing. They did something more. They demonstrated their faith and the man's faith in a bold and practical way. They elbowed their way through the crowd, climbed on top of a house, tore open the roof, and placed their paralyzed friend right in front of Jesus' face!

Perhaps today there is someone in your life you can place right in front of Jesus for His mercy. Whatever the need, Jesus is the One Who supplies. As in today's reading, He is the Healer. He is the Savior. Jesus is also the One Who gives wisdom about the affairs of our lives: our relationships, career choices, and our daily schedules. In His compassion and love for us, He tells us to be bold and persistent in coming to him with our requests. (Hebrews 4:16)

Just as the paralyzed man and his friends exercised great faith in Jesus' power to heal, we too can be bold in our faith that Jesus will have mercy and help our friends, and even ourselves. We too can demonstrate our faith in practical ways. We can let others know we care by our prayers and the acts of kindness we perform toward them. We can take them to Jesus and show them the Savior.

JOURNAL THE ISSUE:

In the space below, write the names of the people the Lord has put on your heart for prayer. Opposite the names, jot down specific ways you can be of practical service to them. Then, do what the Lord says to do.

_____

_____

PRAYER:

Dear Lord, sometimes I let petty obstacles keep me from telling others about You. Help me to be more like the friends of the paralyzed man and allow nothing to stop me from sharing Your goodness with others. In Jesus' name, I ask. Amen.

DO THE SIMPLE THING

Then went he down, and dipped himself seven times in Jordan, according to the saying of the man of God: and his flesh came again like unto the flesh of a little child, and he was clean. (2 Kings 5:14, KJV)

Read 2 Kings 5:1-13

As a captain of the Syrian Army, Naaman was used to being in control. But Naaman had leprosy. When Naaman sought out the Prophet Elisha for help, Elisha didn't pray over him as Naaman expected. Instead, he sent the instructions for curing his leprosy by his servant. Elisha's solution seemed too simplistic to Naaman. He became insulted, refused to carry out the Prophet's instructions, and turned in anger for home.

As Christians, we are to bear each other's burdens and pray for one another. What great power there is in that! I thank God for prayer warriors who can come beside us with their strength and encouragement.

But there are times when I'm tempted to want to do things my way, like Naaman. This can even extend to my own prayer life. If I'm not careful, I can be enticed to think the answers to my prayers depend on my own flurry of activity to line up just the right spiritual resources: prayer warriors, prayer circles, endless requests for prayer, and so on. I'm tempted to think God won't hear my own weak, solitary prayers, even the unuttered cries of my heart, without the mighty power of many people praying. While there is definitely power in the prayers of many believers praying, God's answers don't depend on how well we can orchestrate these things.

Like Naaman, we can make the mistake of thinking we know what's needed. At times, we need to silence the clatter of our own efforts so we can hear God calling, telling us to do the simple thing. We can miss hearing the Lord's voice saying to come away, alone, to Him so He can show us His grace. In the silence with our hearts before God, there we find the strength and help we need.

JOURNAL THE ISSUES:

1. In the space below, write about a time you wanted God to solve a problem your way but the Lord brought a different solution that was just perfect.

_____

_____

2. What did you learn from that experience that can help for the present and future?

_____

_____

3. List some ways you can encourage someone whose faith might be weak.

_____

_____

PRAYER:

Heavenly Father, sometimes, it's hard to understand how You will bring good out of the tangles in my life. There is so much I think I know. But, my understanding is limited. Help me to have enough faith in You to do the simple things You want me to do. Help me to surrender control of my life and let You direct it as You see fit. Please strengthen my weak faith. In Jesus' name, I pray. Amen.

REMOVE THE SCALES

And Ananias went his way, and entered into the house; and putting his hands on him said, Brother Saul, the Lord, even Jesus, that appeared unto thee in the way as thou camest, hath sent me, that thou mightest receive thy sight, and be filled with the Holy Ghost. And immediately there fell from his eyes as it had been scales: and he received sight forthwith, and arose, and was baptized. (Acts 9:17-18, KJV)

Read Acts 9:17-18 and Acts 22:12-13

When the Lord blinded Saul of Tarsus, it was a dramatic event and in full view of all. Saul, who was once in complete control, was now sightless and unable to find his way. The men with him had to lead him around. At God's word, Ananias touched Saul and the Bible says something like scales fell from his eyes. He was no longer blind.

We might have the gift of physical sight, but we can still be blind. We can be spiritually blind. We can fail to see areas of sin in our lives and the way God is working within us. We can be unable to see clearly God's love for us and others and His desire for our affection. Not being able to see clearly through the fog of the lies our Enemy tells us can stunt our spiritual growth and lead us deeper into sin. We need God to remove the scales from our eyes so we can truly see what He is showing us.

During a personal crisis, those around me prayed that the Lord would change my situation for the better and that I would forgive everyone involved. They even prayed for the ones who had hurt me. But that was not a prayer in which I would take part. Instead of joining in that prayer, I wanted to lash out at my oppressors with the same painful actions and words they had shown toward me. I wanted them to feel the same pain I felt. I knew I should forgive but I stubbornly refused. I was blind to my own hardened heart.

Gradually, the Lord removed the scales from my eyes and I came face to face with the sin I was harboring. Unable to hide behind my blind spots any longer, I cried out to God to forgive me of pride and resentment and to help me to forgive the other parties. True forgiveness of deep hurts is not always a quick process. It takes the scouring of the Holy Spirit to break through the calloused shell of deep-rooted hostility. But the cleansing power of Jesus' love washes away all residue of enmity.

JOURNAL THE ISSUE:

1. Has the Holy Spirit nudged you recently about certain "blind spots" in your life? Note them here:

_____

_____

2. Pick one of them. Ask the Lord how you might cooperate with Him in making changes to those areas of your life. Record your insights here.

_____

_____

3. Seek out someone else to hold you accountable in this area.

_____

_____

PRAYER:

Heavenly Father, thank You for revealing truth to me about myself. Without Your Spirit moving within me, I am blind to my own faults. I ask that You open my spiritual eyes so I can see the ways You are working in me. Renew me in those deep places that I try to keep hidden—even from You. I ask in Jesus' name. Amen.

NEGATIVE WORK ENVIRONMENT

"My God hath sent his angel, and hath shut the lions' mouths, that they have not hurt me: forasmuch as before him innocency was found in me...." (Daniel 6:22a, KJV)

Read Daniel 6: 12-28

Daniel knew a thing or two about negative and hostile work environments. Daniel was more than 80 years old and had spent most of his life serving three different Babylonian kings. He had been "set up" repeatedly by jealous coworkers, but each time he triumphed over their evil schemes. Plots to sabotage him dogged him day and night. His enemies could find no fault with his character or his work. Through trickery, they convinced the king to ban any prayer that didn't worship the King. The punishment for disobedience—the lions' den.

Some modern workplaces are not much different. Covetous coworkers may try to take credit for our ideas or try to disrupt our efforts. Some may mock us because of our love for Jesus. Even our supervisors may not understand us. But, if we do find ourselves in a negative workplace, the lesson we can learn from Daniel is that placing our entire trust in God, regardless of workplace conditions, yields untold rewards. The way Daniel responded is the way we should want to respond if we're ever in similar circumstances. When he heard of his coworkers' schemes, Daniel didn't panic, storm in to see the king, or even ask God to get revenge on his behalf. Instead, he prayed to God and gave thanks to God, *as he always did.* What confidence and faith in God!

As Jesus was dying on the cross for our sins, He went even further and asked God to forgive His tormentors. It's the same step we must take. We ask God to forgive those who come against us; but we also ask God to help us to forgive our oppressors.

JOURNAL THE ISSUE:

Here's an exercise you can do if you find yourself (or if you know someone who is) in a negative work environment.

1. Make two lists, one list of people or situations you agree with, the other of the people or situations you disagree with. Then, think about how you can pray for the people and circumstances on both lists.

_____

_____

2. Write your prayer points below; hold these people and situations up to the Lord during your quiet times until the situation changes. If you're not yet ready to pray for those you disagree with, or who disagree with you, ask the Lord for forgiveness and to soften your heart.

_____

_____

PRAYER:

Heavenly Father, thank you for my job and the skills and abilities You've given that enable me to do my job. Bless those You've placed to work side by side with me, even those with whom I may disagree. Help me to have a forgiving heart toward anyone who has wronged me. Please send Your Holy Spirit to intervene and bring peace and forgiveness to the situation. In Jesus' name, I pray. Amen.

UNSEEN HELPERS

...behold the mountain was full of horses and chariots of fire round about Elisha. (2 Kings 6:17, KJV)

Read 2 Kings 6:14-17; Psalm 34:7

One morning, I was driving on the freeway to my job, 25 miles away from my home. It had snowed a few days earlier but there was still ice on the road in some places. I was in the middle lane at the height of rush-hour traffic. Suddenly, several large cardboard boxes loomed in front of my car, partially in my lane. I had no way of knowing whether the boxes were empty or not. It took mere seconds for me to see the boxes, decide against driving over them at 55 miles per hour, check my right-hand mirror to make sure the next lane was empty, and to turn the steering wheel slightly to bypass the boxes. Unknowingly, I turned onto a patch of ice on the ground.

Spinning helplessly out of control with four lanes of traffic behind me, I instinctively cried out, "Jesus, save me!" When my car stopped spinning, it was turned backward, and I was staring into the faces of the drivers who had been behind me. Every car in every lane was completely stopped and evenly lined up, as if some heavenly hand had dropped an invisible curtain between them and me. No one was hurt. No cars were damaged. And my car had just swerved 180 degrees at 55 miles per hour!

Shaken, I managed to turn the car back around to face it in the right direction and pull off the road. I was too frightened to drive. As the enormity of the situation began to sink in, I could only give thanks to God.

Elisha's prayer for his servant is inspiring and challenging at the same time. He didn't pray for the Lord to send a heavenly host to protect them or to surround them, the way I sometimes pray. As shown in the scriptures above, they were already there, carrying out the Lord's bidding.

Whether or not we are aware of our unseen helpers, it is enough for us to know that they are there. And it is more than enough to know that Jesus is present with us at all times. The enemy of our souls wishes to do us harm, but as Elisha said, "…they that be with us are more than they that be with them." (2 Kings 6:16, KJV) With the resources of heaven and earth at His disposal, God is not limited in how He chooses to work. Whether through divine revelation as with Elisha's servant or through ordinary circumstances, we can take comfort that our Heavenly Father is watching over us and is guiding us in the direction He wants us to go.

JOURNAL THE ISSUE:

Think about some of the ways the Lord has recently guided you and what the outcome was. How does this knowledge affect your faith in God's goodness and plan for your life?

_____

_____

PRAYER:

Lord, please open my spiritual eyes today to the human helpers you've assigned to me and to the many ways You guide me. Remind me to thank them; they do their best to make life better for me. In a small way, they are representing You. Show me how I can be of special help to someone today. I ask this in the name of Your Son Jesus. Amen.

HELPING TO HEAL THE EARTH

And he went forth unto the spring of the waters, and cast the salt in there, and said, Thus saith the LORD, I have healed these waters; there shall not be from thence any more death or barren land. (2 Kings 2:21, KJV)

Read 2 King 2:19-22

Global warming, killer storms, acid rain, fossil-fuel pollution. Some years ago, not many people had even heard of these terms, let alone were concerned about their effects. Now, just about everyone has some idea of what these terms mean. Whichever side of the environmental debate we stand, we have to admit that God expects us to take care of the earth, as noted in Genesis 1:28 and elsewhere in the Bible.

This was brought to my attention recently when I learned about extraordinary efforts some are making to right some of the abuses mankind has bestowed upon the earth. I am intrigued, even inspired, when I learn about the thousands of people who remove trash and debris out of our rivers. When I hear of numerous people, including schoolchildren, who regularly clean debris from our streams and river banks, I'm encouraged that perhaps we can make a change in the present state of affairs. With the current emphasis on living "green," this just might happen.

I don't pretend to have it all together when it comes to this issue. I've taken some small steps, but I'm beginning to think I need to step it up a bit. The point is that we can all do a better job of taking care of the earth. We can work on our own or with our civic and other organizations to clean up the place. We can fulfill the mandate God gave us. "And God blessed them, and God said unto them, Be fruitful, and multiply, and replenish the earth, and subdue it: and have dominion over the fish of the sea, and over the fowl of the air, and over every living thing that moveth upon the earth." (Genesis 1:28, KJV) With each of us doing our part, our children and, perhaps even we ourselves may be able to see renewal in the earth.

JOURNAL THE ISSUE:

Think about some of the things you are doing now (or can begin to do in the future) to help heal the earth. Note some of them here.

_____

_____

PRAYER:

Heavenly Father, I need to do more to respect the earth that You gave us. Help me to do my part. Please help me to move forward from where I am right now and do my share in taking better care of the resources You've given. In Jesus' name, I pray. Amen.

LOOK BEYOND MERE SIGHT

But when they saw him walking upon the sea, they supposed it had been a spirit, and cried out: For they all saw him, and were troubled. And immediately he talked with them, and saith unto them, Be of good cheer: it is I; be not afraid. (Mark 6:49-50, KJV)

Read Mark 6:48-52

In this passage the disciples had just left the mountain where Jesus had performed one of His greatest miracles—the feeding of 5,000 men from five loaves of bread and two fish. The disciples saw it with their own eyes. By now, surely they must have known that Jesus was no ordinary man. Surely now they recognized Him as the Messiah, for only the Messiah could do the things Jesus had done. But, the Bible says that when they saw Jesus walking on the sea near their ship, they didn't think about the feeding of the 5,000 that had just taken place, because their hearts were hardened. (Mark 6:52) They were unwilling to believe. In their confusion of trying to fit the irrational into the footprint of the rational, their only explanation for what they were seeing is that it had to be a ghost.

It's amazing that almost immediately after performing one of the great miracles of His ministry, Jesus' disciples failed to believe their Master was capable of another equally miraculous feat. They had seen Him defy the laws of nature before. Still, they wouldn't believe. We certainly can't say that we're any better than the disciples. We would have responded in a similar manner. But the steadying voice of the Lord says to us also, "Be of good cheer: it is I, be not afraid." (Mark 6:50)

Jesus wants us to look beyond what we see with our eyes and beyond what we think we know with our minds. He wants us to focus on Him and His great love for us. As a divorced mother raising my children alone, there have been many times I could only see doom and gloom. An unexpected tax bill, a trip to the emergency room, an angry teacher's call about a child, a friend's betrayal, and other upsets, can all threaten to harden our hearts to the Lord's past faithfulness and bring paralyzing fear. When we reach for Him from this deep place, the spirit of God meets us and fills us with faith and courage. His desire is for us to move to that deep place at the core of our being where He is, where we can find His healing, His refreshing, and His rest.

You may be in a situation where you're trying to make some changes in your life. Maybe you're trying to recover from a setback or move forward in some way. All you can see are the obstacles in front of you.

The Lord Almighty understands our situation intimately and wants the best for us. He is the God of the impossible, the God of miracles. Won't you listen to what the Lord is whispering in your heart? Don't harden your heart. He knows the way ahead and even now is preparing us for it. Trust Him.

JOURNAL THE ISSUE:

1. Are you finding it difficult now to believe God? Briefly, jot down why you think this is the case.

---

2. In a few sentences, write out and rehearse aloud how Jesus helped you in the past. Keep reminding yourself of that several times during the next few weeks until it fills your spirit, with faith for the present.

PRAYER:

Heavenly Father, I need your help to overcome my doubts and fears. Take me back to the foot of the cross where You demonstrated Your great power to cleanse me from doubt and disbelief. In Jesus' name, I pray. Amen.

USE WHAT YOU HAVE

Then he said, Go, borrow thee vessels abroad of all thy neighbours, even empty vessels; borrow not a few. (2 Kings 4:3, KJV)

Read 2 Kings 4:1-7

Sometimes we can be so focused on what we think we don't have that we forget all about God's provision for us. I know people who are always drawing attention to what they don't have. They say they don't have enough money to do this or that, or enough time, or enough energy. They say they're not smart enough, or they can't do it because they never had anyone to show them how or to encourage them, and on and on with the excuses. All of that may be true, but they seem to have forgotten something of utmost importance—they've forgotten God. Without even recognizing it, we all have natural abilities, resources, and hidden treasures that the Lord has placed in us to achieve the things that can sustain our lives and, at the same time, accomplish His purposes on the earth for us. It's true today and it was true many years ago.

A woman's husband died, leaving her with two children and much debt. A creditor threatened to make her and her sons work off what she owed him. The woman was frantic because her two sons were all she had. There was no local convenience store where she could get a job to make ends meet. To her, what she did have looked as if it were nothing. Fear and desperation blinded her to the potential of the resources within her own home. Working through the Prophet Elisha, God provided for her and her children in a miraculous way. And God took her beyond anyplace she might have imagined. She became a businesswoman of a commodity that everyone needed: oil. She learned to set her price, negotiate with her customers, pay her debts, and have enough for her and her sons to live on. God turned her desperation into joy.

What happens when you've reached a crisis point, when you can see no end to the crisis or no way out? What do you do when all your resources seem to amount to nothing except "a pot of oil." (2 Kings 4:2, KJV) During these days of downsizings, threatened foreclosures, and financial stress, it's easy to look at our own meager resources and despair. God has a path for you that may be different from anything you might have imagined.

Let's look to our Provider, our Heavenly Father. He sees all our needs, even our unrecognized needs, and provides for them in astounding and amazing ways! Take heart from this single mother's story and the Lord's care for you.

JOURNAL THE ISSUE:

Make a list of your interests, talents, skills, and abilities, no matter how insignificant and small you think they are. (If needed, use a separate sheet of paper.) Hold them up to the Lord in prayer. Opposite each item, note how you can develop them further for your own livelihood, to help others, and for the glory of God.

_____

_____

PRAYER:

Father, thank You for the abilities and interests You gave me when You created me. Help me to use them all in ways that point others to Jesus and lift Your name on high. In Jesus' name, I pray. Amen.

STORMY WEATHER

And he was in the hinder part of the ship, asleep on a pillow: and they awake him, and say unto him, Master, carest thou not that we perish? And he arose, and rebuked the wind, and said unto the sea, Peace, be still. And the wind ceased, and there was a great calm. (Mark 4:38-39, KJV)

Read Mark 4:35-41

I was six years old when it happened, but I still remember the incident. School had let out and I had to wait for my mother to pick me up. I always waited in the same place, under the big tree by the bus stop. In those days, it was highly unlikely that someone would harm a child who was alone. Mama worked a short bus ride from the school and normally I only had to wait a few minutes before she arrived.

However, this day was different. I was at my usual place at the bus stop at the corner of the school, waiting under the big tree when a violent thunderstorm arose. The storm must have slowed down traffic, making her bus run behind schedule. There were no cell phones to call ahead. I was soaked and frightened. Mama was nowhere in sight.

Then, a kind elderly woman with an open umbrella crossed the street to where

I stood under the tree and persuaded me to come inside her house, out of the rain, to wait for my mother. I remember she told me it was not safe under the tree in the storm. We both watched for my mother from the woman's living room window. Somehow, I must have trusted her.

At every turn during His ministry on earth, Jesus asked His disciples to trust him. When getting into the boat, He told them they were going to the other side of the lake. While doing just that—going over to the other side—a violent storm arose without warning. The Bible tells that the storm was so violent that waves covered the boat and the disciples thought they were going to drown. But Jesus, Who had just miraculously healed many people, demonstrated to the disciples that He also ruled over the seas and could stop the storm with just a word.

Perhaps you are in the midst of a personal storm and you're frightened by the things you see and hear. Your particular storm might be a job loss, a health challenge, a wayward child, or a spiritual crisis. Everywhere you turn, giant waves of disaster threaten to sink your hope—even your faith. You've tried holding on, but you're beginning to lose your grip. Maybe you've taken things into your own hands and merely made a mess. Even your prayers seem like sawdust in your mouth. And like the disciples in today's reading, you're wondering if God really cares about you, why doesn't He do something?

This is the time to hold onto Jesus with everything you have through sustained prayer. It doesn't matter how fierce the wind or how high the waves of disaster are. We know Jesus, Who created the universe, is in control of all that pertains to us.

JOURNAL THE ISSUE:

1. Sometimes we say we're trusting God for everything concerning us. Yet, is that always true? If we completely trusted all areas of our lives to God, would our lives now be different? Explain below.

_____

_____

2. Make a list of some of the areas where you know you need to trust Jesus more.

_____

_____

PRAYER:

I give up, Lord! I give up trying to find my way through the storms of life without Your help. I go astray so many times when I take my life into my own hands. I trust You and turn myself over to You completely, even trusting You when the way ahead is not clear.

IT'S ALL ABOUT OBEDIENCE

And Simon answering said unto him, Master, we have toiled all the night, and have taken nothing: nevertheless at thy word I will let down the net. And when they had this done, they enclosed a great multitude of fishes: and their net brake. And they beckoned unto their partners, which were in the other ship, that they should come and help them. And they came, and filled both the ships, so that they began to sink. (Luke 5:6-7, KJV)

Read Luke 5:1-11

My Great Auntie was very much old school. She lived during an era when women dipped snuff or smoked corncob pipes, and decent women didn't wear makeup. Sometimes when she wanted to make a point, she'd tell me about her life before she knew Christ. And she was definitely making a point to me on that particular day. No doubt, she detected the smell of cigarettes on my new college-girl clothes as I stood in her living room. She told me of a time when she used to dip snuff.

What? I couldn't believe it! It was not possible that this straight-laced, church-going Christian woman had ever allowed tobacco to cross her lips! Yet, it was true. She told me that after she committed her life to Jesus, she searched the Bible for any prohibitions against dipping snuff. She said she didn't find anything in the Bible against it but she thought the Lord wouldn't like it. So she quit. Just like that. She never said another word to me about it, or about my smoking. But, I got her point.

Later, when I came to know the Lord for myself, I had a similar decision to make—the Holy Spirit within was telling me to stop smoking. I had to obey. I had to face the fact that the Bible says my body is the temple of the Lord. (I Corinthians 6:19) It was the same choice Great Auntie had to make years earlier. Though the circumstances were vastly different, it was the same choice we see Peter making in today's Scripture—the choice to obey God, despite what he thought he knew. We may not know immediately the full outcome of our choices to obey God, but we do know that He considers obedience crucial to our relationship with him. And obedience brings a reward.

JOURNAL THE ISSUE:

Describe what the Holy Spirit is saying to you from today's passage about obedience.

_____

_____

PRAYER:

Heavenly Father, as a creature of flesh, I'm so weak. I don't do the things I should and I do the things I shouldn't. How I need Your help! By the power of Jesus' shed blood, make me stronger. Help me be consistent in my desire to live for You. In Jesus' name, I pray. Amen.

MIRACULOUS LANDING

But when he saw the wind boisterous, he was afraid; and beginning to sink, he cried, saying, Lord, save me. (Matthew 14:30, KJV)

Read Matthew 14:26-32

When Peter walked on the water toward Jesus, he was filled with faith. But after a few seconds he took his eyes off Jesus. He saw the rolling waves, became afraid, and began to sink into the water. And the Lord chastised him because of his lack of faith.

We have to believe that the airline pilot who landed his crippled plane in the Hudson River was also filled with faith. When he landed his jetliner on the waters of the Hudson, the plane floated, thereby saving dozens of lives. The media immediately dubbed the story a miracle because of its miraculous outcome.

Like Peter, this pilot wasn't afraid to take a chance. He threw away the rulebook and gambled at a never-tried-before landing. Rather than settle for a known outcome—the massive loss of life that could occur by trying to ditch his plane on land—he reached out for the unknown. He landed his jetliner on top of the waters of the Hudson River. Although the decision looked like certain death, his daring and God's mercy brought about a good resolution.

I know nothing about the pilot's faith, but I like to think that his faith in God was at least equal to his faith in his own piloting skills. I like to think that in those last few moments that were almost too quick to measure, he determined to use every skill he had as a pilot and inwardly call upon God to make up for what he lacked. I like to think that the earnest, collective prayers of the passengers and crew united in one accord and stormed the very gates of heaven. And God honored their faith. Only God can perform a miracle—whether or not it's recognized as such by the media or the public. God was with them that day, and kept them all safe through His loving kindness.

This side of heaven, we can't be certain of the full reasons this flight was spared while some others are not. Such things are not for us to know. God reserves those answers for Himself. Though we don't have all the answers, we do know that God is good. We do know He is filled with tender mercies and compassion. The Bible says the Lord's compassions are "new every morning" (Lamentations 3:23a, KJV) and His love knows no bounds. This is what we hold in our hearts as we meditate on the miracles of God.

JOURNAL THE ISSUES:

1. Make a note of a time you had to take a chance or make a split-second decision about something that might have been controversial or dangerous.

_____

_____

2. What was the outcome? Looking back, explain why it was or was not a good decision.

_____

_____

3. Write what the Holy Spirit is telling you about taking a chance for the Lord.

_____

_____

PRAYER:

Heavenly Father, sometimes what looks like certain disaster to us is really Your way of bringing blessings into our lives. In these uncertain times, help me to be willing to take a chance, to risk everything for Your sake. In Jesus' name, I pray. Amen.

A DREAM DEFERRED OR GOD'S TIMING?

And Pharaoh said unto Joseph, See, I have set thee over all the land of Egypt. (Genesis 41:41, KJV)

Read Genesis 41:37-49

In the Bible, Joseph lived for many years with big dreams in his heart. He was only 17 when he told his brothers of the dreams of leadership the Lord had given him. Instead of being elevated as he thought he'd be, his jealous brothers sold him into slavery where he was thrown into prison for many years. What a seemingly cruel and harsh fate. He must have wondered where God was during all that time. Unknown to Joseph, God had placed him in a unique position where he would save many lives from famine, including the lives of his own family.

Many women live with unfulfilled hopes and dreams that the Lord has given: dreams to marry and have children, dreams to open a business, to travel, to do ministry work, or the like. Some have legitimate reasons for not taking action on their dreams: they might be a homemaker with small children or the sole support of the family. Physical impairments may limit what some can do. But many of us simply make excuses for our lack of action. I'm certainly no exception!

Imagine what would happen if we all determined to hold onto and act on the dreams the Lord has put in our hearts! If we don't have that kind of determination now, we can ask the Lord to strengthen us so that we do have that resolve.

Sometimes when we think we've given our all in acting on our dream, we'll suddenly meet a roadblock. Disappointment, discouragement, and doubt can overwhelm us. If we let it. It's during these times we need to remember God has His own timing for the events in our lives—just as He did for Joseph. We need to hold onto our dreams, continue working toward them but leave the timing of their fulfillment to the Lord.

God gives us hopes and dreams as He sees fit and brings them to pass in the manner and timing according to His will.

So, keep your dream before the Lord and in your heart. But, do more than just keep it in your heart. Unless the Lord says no, begin to act on it. Seek the Lord for the right timing. Take the first step, then the second. Keep at it with humility and faith until the dream in your heart meshes with God's plan for your life.

JOURNAL THE ISSUES:

Write down some of the hopes and dreams the Lord has put in your heart over the years. Note which ones have been fulfilled and what action is needed to make the others a reality. In prayer, ask the Lord for wisdom to do the things He wants you to do.

_____

_____

PRAYER:

Heavenly Father, I bring my hopes and dreams to You. Set them aright, according to Your divine plan. Help me to know how to do what is right in Your eyes and according to Your timing. In Jesus' name, I ask. Amen.

KILLER LIGHTS

Is anything too hard for the Lord? (Genesis 18:14, KJV)

Read Genesis 18:9-15

Some years ago, before children had to be strapped in car seats for safety reasons, I drove through a long tunnel with my toddler in the back seat. When I glanced toward the back seat at the strange noises coming from him, he was crouched on all fours on the back seat, whimpering like a scared puppy. Heavy traffic made it impossible to stop. I swiveled the rear view mirror so it was trained fully on him.

He moaned something about the lights hitting his head, and then he rolled off the seat onto the floor. Unable to tell what had frightened him, I quickly glanced at the cars around us, then straight ahead. That's when I understood.

As I drove through the tunnel, the ceiling lights formed an inverted "V" that seemed to rush straight for my head: "killer lights." To a young child riding for the first time in a tunnel at 55 miles per hour, the danger of the overhead lights must have seemed quite real. Despite my attempts to reassure him, it wasn't until we were out of the tunnel and in full daylight that he felt safe enough to climb back on the seat.

Sometimes our faith in God is a little like that. We see the obstacles ahead, whether real or imaginary. As the obstacles in our lives rush toward us and threaten to destroy us, our first reaction may be to hide in fear. Instead of listening to God and the assurances He gives us, we listen to the rising panic in our own hearts. Sarah, Abraham's wife, laughed in derision and fear when she heard the Lord say she'd have a son. She couldn't get past the fact that she and Abraham were physically too old to have a child. But God, Who is rich in mercy and true to His Word, performed a great miracle in their bodies. Sarah soon gave birth to Isaac, who began the fulfillment of God's promises to Abraham for a great nation.

When we are weak, it seems as if everything frightens us. Our Enemy tempts us to give more power to the obstacles we see than to God's promises. But we can remember God's promise to never fail us during our time of need. We can be confident that He will help us <u>because</u> we trust in Him.

JOURNAL THE ISSUES:

1. Do you know someone whose faith and trust in God seems to be faltering? Write their name below. Pray first, and then try reaching out to encourage that person according to the Lord's leading. Remind them that God will not leave them helpless. If we call on Him in prayer, He has promised to answer.

_____

_____

2. Genesis 18:14 asks, "Is anything too hard for the Lord?" Believe that the Lord will help you find ways to reach out to that person. Note some of them below.

_____

_____

PRAYER:

Heavenly Father, my friend seems so burdened with problems. Her faith seems weak. I feel so powerless to help her. Please put Your arms around her and show her anew Your powerful love and care for her. Use me to encourage her. I ask this in Jesus' name. Amen.

KEEP STEPPING

And she said, As the LORD thy God liveth, I have not a cake, but an handful of meal in a barrel, and a little oil in a cruse: and, behold, I am gathering two sticks, that I may go in and dress it for me and my son, that we may eat it, and die. (1 Kings 17:12, KJV)

Read 1 Kings 17:8-16

Things in our country look really bad right now. The news from Wall Street can be scary. Everywhere there's talk of coming ruin and destruction, as there surely was during the times of the drought in this scripture passage. Because of today's economy, your job, or your husband's, might be terminated. You're worried about finding a way to help support your family. You're scared you might lose the house. To make matters worse, the car is giving trouble and you're having conflicts with a long-time friend. Can things get any worse?

That's a tough spot to be in. All of us go through times when major life crises seem to knock us over. We say to ourselves that if we have to deal with one more problem, we're going to scream. The truth is that the chances are high that we <u>will</u> have to deal with one or more crises eventually.

It's just part of the human existence. But, look up! The suffering Jesus endured put an end to our helplessness in the face of a crisis. When life events knock us to the ground, there's only one thing to do. Cry out to God, get back up, and keep stepping onward. Keep going. Persevere, knowing that the Spirit of God gives us the strength to keep doing what we know we need to do. If we need to cry, we cry, but we don't give up. Though it may seem as if we're in the pits right now, we know there is an upside. The upside is that we've weathered similar storms in the past; by God's grace, we've managed to come through them. The upside is that we are not in this situation alone; God is right here with us. We also learned a few things from past upsets that can help us overcome the next set of obstacles life throws our way.

The greatest lessons we can learn as Christians is to rely on and obey God, as the woman in today's Scripture did. Something inside her knew she'd heard the voice of God through Elijah. She didn't ask why or how. She just obeyed God. She didn't give up. She had done all she could do to care for herself and her son, and unless the Lord intervened they would starve to death. God's words from the Prophet shot great faith through her that God was with her, despite her circumstances.

Raising two children on my own, I had to learn to depend on the Lord instead of other people. The Lord taught me to tamp down the rising feelings of fear and panic that threatened to engulf me. Everything within me screamed, "Just give up!" But, somebody had to take care of the children and keep things going. I was that somebody. Perhaps you are that person for your family, or you know someone who is.

Only God's grace allowed me to keep stepping, to keep moving forward.

During that dark time, the Lord sat beside me and taught me how to move from today's despair to tomorrow's hope. Here are some of the things He taught me.

Daily Bible reading and Scripture memory. My needs were so great that I spent large chunks of time searching the Bible and crying out daily in prayer to the Lord for help—where to find a better job, where to get my car fixed, what to do about loneliness, and so on. And the Lord heard and answered my cries through amazing "coincidences:" an agency offered a job at a better salary based on an application I had forgotten about. The Lord can, and I believe will, set up amazing "coincidences" for you also. Bible reading and memorizing Scripture puts, and keeps, us in touch with the Lord, His goodness and His promises. (Exodus 34:6)

Quiet time with the Lord. Meeting alone daily with the Lord in the mornings brought new insight and wisdom. My idea of God as frowning and angry changed as a result. Little by little, He taught me about Himself and His care for me. And, bit by bit, step by step, I learned to recognize and follow His guidance. As I spent more time with the Lord, my panic began to subside and He filled me with assurances of His care.

Prayer journal. A written record of answered prayer showed me that I could trust His guidance. When praying about funds to pay the bills, a refund check for almost the exact amount needed arrived unexpectedly in the mail. When at a loss at how to parent my child, during daily Bible reading the answer seemed to jump off the page at me. Inspired by that great time of need in my life, I still keep a written record of prayer requests and the Lord's answers. Keeping a written record of God's faithful answers to prayer over time has been powerful encouragement to me and countless others. Seeing His trustworthiness in the past, we know He's faithful to help us step over whatever hurdles the present and the future may bring.

As believers, we keep moving toward the place the Lord calls us to, toward the actions He wants us to take. With the Lord on our side, we *can* keep moving forward. Even if we take a wrong turn, He is faithful to bring us gently back where we belong.

JOURNAL THE ISSUES:

1. Note a few instances when you've had to keep moving forward despite extraordinary odds.

_____

_____

2. What does it mean to you to know that God is with you during life's struggles? Why can't the Christian simply give up or become complacent?

_____

_____

PRAYER:

Heavenly Father, sometimes I feel the struggle is too much for me. Please give me the courage to continue on the path You've set for me and the strength to follow You till the end. In Jesus' name, I ask. Amen.

GOD'S PLAN FOR OUR LIVES

For I know the thoughts that I think toward you, saith the LORD, thoughts of peace, and not of evil, to give you an expected end. (Jeremiah 29:11, KJV)

Read Jeremiah 29:11-14

Someone said that the unexamined life is not worth living. Every year, millions of people examine their lives, decide that some change is needed, and make New Year's resolutions. A few months later, most folks have broken or forgotten all about them. Not to be outdone, some others say their resolution is to not make resolutions. They contend that making resolutions is useless because we always break them.

After many years of failed attempts, a woman I know started keeping and reviewing a list of her resolutions, as a way of trying to keep up with them. Eventually, she succeeded with several of them. Sometimes, the resolutions she was able to keep appeared on her list over and over for a period of several years. It can take sustained effort to achieve a long-held goal.

There's wisdom in setting lasting plans and goals for our lives. But did you know that God also makes plans for our lives?

As noted in today's passage, He knows the thoughts and plans he's made for each of us. Ephesians 1:4 says He made plans for us individually before He created the earth.

How can this be? What an amazing truth: that God planned ahead of time to save us, to forgive our sins through Jesus' death on the cross. When the time is right, the Lord himself will also reveal Himself to us. What an honor to cooperate with God's thoughts and plans for our lives. As shown above, His plans are filled with divine mercy and goodness.

When we don't seek the Lord's guidance, our own worldly plans can interfere with God's plans for us, and our lives can end up in a muddle. But, I believe He uses even our biggest fumbles to further His grand plan. We don't always know or understand how God will bring good out of the tragedies in our lives. We're perplexed to imagine how, for example, lives devastated by natural disasters or other calamities can be worked for good. But God knows. When we seek Him in the face of catastrophe, He gives us peace in knowing that He's able to turn things around for our good. We don't see how this can be, but we can take comfort knowing His thoughts and plans for good are constantly directed toward us. Because He is good. Trouble may enter our lives and plans may go awry; but we can cry mightily to the Lord to put us back on the path He has for us. What a loving heavenly father we have!

JOURNAL THE ISSUES:

Make a list of some of the mistakes you made in life that threatened to be disastrous. Opposite each one, jot down how the Lord either turned it into good for His glory or is presently doing so. Also, note what the Lord is saying to you through that experience.

_____

_____

PRAYER:

Heavenly Father, thank You for the plans You have for every detail of our lives. Help me to live with confidence knowing that You can turn even my errors into mighty testaments of Your great power, goodness, and love. In Jesus' name, I pray. Amen.

LESSONS FROM THE BED

And he leaping up stood, and walked, and entered with them into the temple, walking, and leaping, and praising God. And all the people saw him walking and praising God.... (Acts 3:8-9, KJV)

Read Acts 3:1-11

"How ironic," I thought, after surgery. "There I was trying to extend the love of Jesus to a sick friend. Now, here I am, flat on my back, fighting nausea, unable to walk."

When I found out a friend was ill, I wanted to do everything I could to help her recover. But something as insignificant as going down a flight of stairs caused the cartilage in my knee to tear. A few weeks later, I was the one who was in the hospital.

I didn't want to hear it when my doctor told me that I needed surgery. The idea of going under anesthesia and through surgery was frightening to me. I didn't want the downtime required. I thought I was too busy to be laid up because of illness. I was totally unprepared for the events that followed. The doctors told me arthroscopic surgery was the way to go—minimal scarring, minimal invasion, faster recovery. All that is true.

But, I didn't know that with knee surgery, you have to learn how to walk all over again!

Four months of physical therapy trained and strengthened my muscles. Strong hands and encouraging words at the parallel bars helped me to keep trying. Tough therapists prodded and kneaded tight muscles. Many days, I left therapy feeling worse than when I arrived. I know now that all this is part of the recovery. Little by little, the soreness lessened, muscles loosened, tendons glided into place, and I began to develop a familiar stride.

That time was not an easy time and it still isn't, for my recovery continues. But, here are some of the lessons the Lord began teaching me, and that I'm still learning.

- *Don't take your good health for granted.* Things can change in the blink of an eye. When I was leaving home, I had no inkling I would be returning home with an injury.
- *Cry out to God for mercy for yourself and others.* It is the God of mercy who sustains us. In His goodness and compassion, Jesus shows His mercy toward us and urges us to have compassion toward others. Matthew 5:7 reminds us, "Blessed are the merciful: for they shall obtain mercy." (KJV)
- *Put independence and pride aside. Lean on others and on God.* Very independent, I was always the one helping others. I had to swallow my

pride and accept the kindness of relatives, friends, and even strangers to help with things I could no longer do for myself. Several months later, there are times when I am still a bit unsteady on my feet and sometimes walk with a cane. That, in itself, is humbling. Having a complete stranger see my cane and hold the door open for me is even more humbling. Watching them walk away at a fast clip is also humbling, as I think, "I used to be able to walk fast like that."

- *Healing is a process.* God can and, I believe, does heal instantly. But, healing is also gradual and is aided immensely by the medical profession and the power of prayer. I'm learning to be patient with the process.

- *Trust God before, during, and afterward. Stay close to God.* I continued to hold up the results to the Lord for a good outcome. I was nervous about the knee surgery, as most people would be. As I prayed about the upcoming procedure, I sensed the Lord whisper His reassurances to me. Those whispered words sustained me before the surgery and were the last thing I remembered as the anesthesia took effect. I wanted God to heal me in a divine, miraculous way. He wanted me to trust Him.
- *Teach others by example.* Even though we may not realize it, others are

watching to see how we react. Some are just waiting for a slipup; others are cheering us on. But, a good many are watching to learn how a Christian handles adversity. Through God's grace, may we teach that lesson well to others.

JOURNAL THE ISSUES:

Note how you've handled adversity in the past. What have you learned from those experiences? What lessons do you think others learned from watching you during trials?

_____

_____

PRAYER:

Heavenly Father, give me the faith that You will help me overcome the unexpected events in my life. May all my words and actions bring honor to You, regardless of the circumstances. In Jesus' name, I pray. Amen.

THE WORLD WAS NOT WORTHY

They were stoned, they were sawn asunder, were tempted, were slain with the sword: they wandered about in sheepskins and goatskins; being destitute, afflicted, tormented, (Of whom the world was not worthy:) they wandered in deserts, and in mountains, and in dens and caves of the earth. (Hebrews 11:37-38, KJV)

Read Hebrews 11:32-40

The story of the growth of Christianity is a miraculous story. From the very beginning, Christians were targets of persecution. The Jews and Romans persecuted Jesus. And Jesus said His followers would also be persecuted.

In *Foxe's Book of Martyrs*, John Foxe, the 16th century author, tells of Christians who were martyred for the faith. William Tyndale, who translated the Bible from Latin to English, was eventually burned at the stake for his translation work. Foxe tells us that with books and teachers in such short supply, it is amazing how the gospel spread as far as it did. Only the hand of God could orchestrate such growth.

Are we passing on the knowledge of God, praying for the lost, sharing our Christian testimonies with others, modeling for our children the qualities they will need as adults? There is no scarcity of books and teachers in our country today. In fact, one could say there's such an abundance that we could be lulled into a sense of false security. But God uses such an abundance to reach as many as will receive Him. Today's Scripture reading says the world was not worthy of those early martyrs. May our generation cherish what they handed down to us. Likewise, may we be faithful to pass the love of Jesus Christ to future generations.

JOURNAL THE ISSUE:

How are we passing on the knowledge of God to others? If we are not doing so now, note below some ways we can begin.

_____

_____

PRAYER:

Heavenly Father, teach us how best to tell others about Jesus. In Jesus' name, I pray. Amen.

PRAY BIG, BOLD PRAYERS

And he said, Thou hast asked a hard thing: nevertheless, if thou see me when I am taken from thee, it shall be so unto thee; but if not, it shall not be so. (2 Kings 2:10, KJV)

Read Acts 9:32-35

When Elijah was about to be taken from the earth, his successor Elisha had a desire for a blessing that was greater than Elijah's. One proof of his desire was his boldness to ask for big things. He knew he couldn't fill Elijah's shoes in his own strength. He'd have to have the courage to ask God for greater blessings than even Elijah had. He could have asked to be like Elijah. Instead, he asked for a double portion of Elijah's anointing. Even Elijah wasn't sure whether God would grant his request or not. But God rewarded Elisha's request in all its boldness.

There were times I think I had a wrong view of God. I tended to make him too small. I tried to fit him into my cup of small expectations. Sometimes, I even thought I was "bothering" God by asking for what I needed. Looking at Elisha's request and at the turnaround in some "impossible" situations, I believe the Lord delights in handling our big, bold requests. I'm learning that praying big prayers to God has the potential to open us up to answers that are far beyond anything we could imagine. God's grace is limitless. Like Elisha, let's pray for the big things, the hard things. Let's ask God to restore that impossible situation, bring peace to that toxic relationship, return that prodigal, heal that dread disease, and reconcile that hopeless individual. When we're faced with situations that seem beyond our reach, that's the time to ask our powerful God to bring His powerful answers into our lives. That's the time to exercise bold faith in Almighty God, and look for His grace toward us and others. Let's continue to pray bold prayers and not give up.

JOURNAL THE ISSUE:

1. Think of a time in your life when you put limits on God's ability to move in significant ways in your life, either because you expected no answer or expected limited results. Note below why you think that was the case.

_____

_____

2. What has God been teaching you about Himself since then?

_____

_____

PRAYER:

Heavenly Father, please open my mind and heart to Your great love and power. Help me to see You as Elisha did—a limitless God who can answer big prayers on behalf of His people. In Jesus' name, I pray. Amen.

WHAT'S NEXT?

But he himself went a day's journey into the wilderness, and came and sat down under a juniper tree: and he requested for himself that he might die; and said, It is enough; now, O LORD, take away my life; for I am not better than my fathers. (1 Kings 19:4, KJV)

Read I Kings 19:1-8

When Jezebel sent a message to Elijah that she was going to kill him, Elijah wasted no time in running for his life. Even as God's instrument in performing the greatest miracle of his life by calling fire down from heaven, Elijah was still shaken by Jezebel's threat. He knew she could do it. As the king's wife, she must have had tremendous power and resources. Elijah was convinced that she had already wiped out God's entire prophetic line, except for him. He thought he was the last of God's prophets and had to stay alive at all costs. Elijah reasoned that if God didn't stop Jezebel from killing 800 prophets, it wasn't likely that the Lord would spare Elijah. He didn't stop to ask God what to do next. He just started running. He was in such a panic that he didn't even remember that God had preserved 100 prophets through the Prophet

Obadiah. Elijah just ran as far and as fast as he could into the wilderness to hide. Finally, after a full day of running, he collapsed in a heap of exhaustion, fear, and depression.

Is this the same man who fearlessly and boldly mocked the prophets of Baal and challenged King Ahab to a contest? Is this the same one who confidently called down fire from heaven? But, a big letdown often rides the heels of great success. After the glow of triumph has faded, we wonder if this is all there is. Or, at the first sign of trouble, we may begin to doubt God's willingness to care for us as he did in the past. We don't stop to seek the Lord's guidance for this new phase or ask Him what the next step is. And neither did Elijah.

We can wrongly think everything depends on us. We can have tremendous faith for the moment, but what about for the long haul? Where is our faith after the cheering crowd has gone home and we're left facing our enemies alone? That was Elijah's situation, and at times, it's also ours.

Has a drastic change in circumstances thrown you into a panic? Perhaps you're distraught over a situation that's deteriorating and you have nowhere to turn.
Instead of running blindly in fear and panic, we can cry out to our Heavenly Father. Our God doesn't leave us to our own devices. As with Elijah, he calls us to Him to rest, receive His care and guidance as to what the next step should be. We can trust Him to be compassionate. God's mercy endures

forever—ask Him to come to your aid and give grace for your situation.

JOURNAL THE ISSUE:

Briefly describe below a time when you were faced with a major life choice and you asked for God's guidance and followed it. Compare that outcome with the outcome for a major choice when you acted totally on your own.

_____

_____

PRAYER:

Lord, like Elijah, sometimes I'm tempted to doubt Your care for me, even after a time of great success. I can be tempted to think that Your care in the past was a one-time occurrence that won't be repeated. Help me to know that I need to seek Your face daily to find out what's next in Your plan for me. In Jesus' name, I pray. Amen.

FORMED ACCORDING TO HIS PURPOSES

For thou hast possessed my reins: thou hast covered me in my mother's womb. (Psalm 139:13, KJV)

Read Psalm 139:13, 15-16, Jeremiah 1:5, and Proverbs 3:1-10

My daughter's heart is tender. I know this because she is always for the underdog. No matter the situation. When she was younger, left to her own devices our house would have become a rescue center for various abandoned, mangy dogs and cats. As she grew older, her feelings for the downtrodden and helpless asserted itself in different ways: though her college major and career choices—an attempt to help those that some in society say are hopeless. And over time, her tender heart was accompanied by a courage that allowed her to make tough decisions.

Where did such concern for others come from? Because I didn't think her job was ultimately good for her, I prayed for the Lord to lead her in another direction. In fact, I did more than that—I let her know in no uncertain terms that I thought she should change careers. She ignored me. I doubled my prayers.

Then, a strange thing happened.

It seemed the Lord dropped into my spirit the thought that He had created her that way. He had created her with this natural bent toward helping others. It was for His purposes, for Him to work out in His own time. Frankly, there was nothing I could do about it.

Sometimes we can be so focused on trying to stamp our own standard on someone that we fail to consider how God is at work in the situation and forget to look for the Lord's purposes.

In a similar way, we may not understand that God might be gently guiding a person's path by putting up barriers around certain pursuits in preparation for the good works he has prepared. Ephesians 2:10 states we were created to perform good works through Jesus Christ.

JOURNAL THE ISSUE:

1. Note any "leanings" your child or another person may demonstrate.

_____

_____

2. Prayerfully ask for wisdom to determine how you can (or even if you should) help that person cultivate those interests. Write what you learn below.

_____

_____

PRAYER:

Heavenly Father, I don't always understand what You have in mind for my loved ones. I don't always know how I can help them. Sometimes, despite my best efforts, I can make things worse. Help me to love them enough to allow You to bring out their best. In Jesus' name, I pray. Amen.

WISDOM IN THE MIDST OF CHAOS

And he touched his ear and healed him. (Luke 22:51b, KJV)

Read Luke 22:47-53

Kneeling in the Garden, Jesus knew what to expect. Evil men would take him away to face His death. One of his companions would betray Him. Another would deny even knowing Him. The others would run away and hide.

In our mind's eye, we can picture a scene of hysteria and confusion in the darkness—the shouts of outrage, fear, anger, hatred, and violence. In the middle of what must have been bedlam, a servant crouches, bleeding and in pain. Jesus, with a rebuke to his disciple, reaches out and administers grace to the servant. What a picture of our Lord: showering compassion and healing to the very ones who came to kill him! Do you think that encounter changed the servant's life?

As a mother, I want to fix everything, to help everyone set things right. As seen in this passage, it's not always wise to react in the heat of the moment, no matter how well-meaning the intention. We need to seek the wisdom of God before moving headlong into situations we don't fully understand. Most of us would probably have reacted in a similar manner as the disciples if we were in that situation. But Jesus had heavenly assistance and opted not to use it. His plan was different. He had a plan, not to save Himself, but to divinely rescue the whole of mankind.

JOURNAL THE ISSUES:

Describe a time when you rushed rashly into a complex situation, without first seeking God's wisdom and without fully understanding all the details. Was the outcome what you thought it would be? What would you have done differently if you had had all the facts?

_____

_____

PRAYER:

Heavenly Father, sometimes I can be too proactive. I rush to do what I think is needed without waiting for Your guidance. Help me learn to temper my desire to "fix" everything, especially when I don't have to do so. In Jesus' name, I pray. Amen.

DON'T OVERLOOK YOUR BLESSINGS

Bless the LORD, O my soul: and all that is within me, bless his holy name. Bless the LORD, O my soul, and forget not all his benefits: Who forgiveth all thine iniquities; who healeth all thy diseases; Who redeemeth thy life from destruction; who crowneth thee with lovingkindness and tender mercies; Who satisfieth thy mouth with good things; so that thy youth is renewed like the eagle's. (Psalm 103:1-5, KJV)

Read Psalm 103

Life isn't always easy. It can become very tough through no fault of our own. The economy tanks and the family business may go under. A loved one may leave or get sick. The person we were depending on may abandon us. At the very least, we're bombarded daily with frightening headlines of impending doom. All of those events are dire. And our Enemy wants us to focus on the negative. We can often become too focused on the negative, too distracted by what we don't have and what we think we need. When that happens, we may miss out on the joys of what the Lord has provided for us and the blessings that come from being God's own special child. Looking at the glamorous lifestyles of others and comparing ourselves to them, we might feel cheated. We forget the friends and family the Lord puts in our lives. He provides for our material needs. However much or little we have, we are thankful, for they are blessings from God. Here are a few of God's blessings we should never overlook:

Life itself. God has given us physical life and the potential for eternal life with him, if we truly believe in His Son and live wholly for Him. Jesus says, "I have come that they may have life, and that they may have it more abundantly." (John 10:10b, KJV)

A measure of good health. All of us cannot be in the best of health all the time, but whatever measure of good health we have at any moment, we praise God for it. "Beloved, I pray that you may prosper in all things and be in health, just as your soul prospers." (3 John 1:2, KJV)

Family and friends. We thank God for the comfort of friends and family, despite their flaws. They love us and stick by us, even when times are tough. God even placed us in a family of believers, as noted in Psalm 68:6:

Hard Things. It may seem contrary to think of misfortunes, the hard things in our lives or the lives of others, as blessings. No one wants to have to deal with troubles. We want to look away from them, avoid them, because they're painful. But often, in the midst of unfortunate events, the Lord teaches us great lessons that draw us even closer to Him and allow us to minister to others in similar situations. "In everything give thanks for this is the will of God in Christ Jesus concerning you." (1 Thessalonians 5:18, KJV)

Ability to praise, sing spiritual songs, and pray. We were made to praise God, pray, and sing spiritual songs to him. What a blessing to be able to commune directly with our Heavenly Father through prayer! Often, the Lord uses our prayers to Him to help us understand Him better and understand what's going on in our own hearts. Praise and spiritual songs to God strengthen our spiritual being and draw us closer to Him. I believe, all this blesses us and, most of all, blesses the Lord by acknowledging Him as our God.

His Spirit. When we are weary, we can look to God for comfort and solace. He sends His Holy Spirit to comfort us and teach us about Himself. God's Spirit sustains us and helps us to become more like Jesus. When we find ourselves genuinely praying for someone who spread malicious gossip about us, for example, rather than exacting revenge, that's the Holy Spirit at work in us. When we can genuinely rejoice at the good things in someone else's life, instead of becoming jealous, that's the Spirit of God affecting us. When we genuinely seek God's presence, that's God's Spirit moving in us.

Jesus' presence. Jesus said He would never leave or forsake us. We can be assured that regardless of what we're going through at the present, He is right there with us. "...I am with you always, even unto the end of the world. Amen." (Matthew 28:20, KJV)

Eternal Life. The greatest blessing of all is also the greatest miracle of them all: the free gift of eternal life through Jesus' death on the cross. Some may see the crucifixion of Jesus as bloody, brutal, vicious, and savage. It was all of that. The Bible says it comes out of the heart of a loving God who knows what is needed far better than we do. Through that event, Jesus endured the penalty for all our sins and promised that those who trust in Him will be with Him throughout eternity. What a miracle blessing from a loving God!

JOURNAL THE ISSUES:

Spend some time meditating on your blessings, and then list all your blessings. Continue on as many sheets of paper as you need.

_____

_____

PRAYER:

Heavenly Father, praise You for the multitude of blessings You send my way daily! Praise You for the gift of eternal life through Your son Jesus! As I go about my activities today, help me to continue to praise you for the blessings You give and the miracle of eternal life through Jesus. In Jesus' name, I pray. Amen.

GIVE GOD YOUR FEARS

Then Mordecai commanded to answer Esther, Think not with thyself that thou shalt escape in the king's house, more than all the Jews. For if thou altogether holdest thy peace at this time, then shall there enlargement and deliverance arise to the Jews from another place; but thou and thy father's house shall be destroyed: and who knoweth whether thou art come to the kingdom for such a time as this? (Esther 4:13-14, KJV)

Read Esther 4:10-5:14

The story of how Queen Esther became such a woman of influence beautifully illustrates some meaningful concepts that we can use in our daily lives. Briefly, this story tells how Esther, a beautiful Jewish woman, won a beauty contest to become the King's wife and, by doing so, was able to save her people from destruction. But Esther had to battle the enemy of fear. If she approached the king and he didn't hold out his golden scepter toward her, she would be executed. After a three-day fast, Esther's faith had grown. It took a brave woman to say before going in front of the king, "If I perish, I perish" (Esther 4:16, KJV).

Reading about the unfolding of Esther's initial reluctance to petition the king for her people reminds me of the doubts and fears many of us harbor: fear of rejection, failure, and even fear of success. Sometimes, we can be afraid we don't have what it takes to answer God's call, or that the Lord hasn't fully equipped us to accomplish His purposes. Like Esther, we, too, can be afraid to fail. Our fears can give rise to mountains of procrastination and discouragement. Pretty soon, we're so bound up in fear that we convince ourselves that we will fail. We give up on the very things we know we should do. We end up in disobedience to God.

Through fasting, prayer, and meditating on the Scriptures, we can come into greater trust in God. We can know that if God calls us to accomplish something, He has already given us the resources we need. Once we begin to trust God, He will cause our fears to subside and open the doors He wants us to enter. We will probably always wrestle with some feelings of uncertainty; it seems to be part of the human condition. Yet, when we soak up familiar Bible stories of those who trusted God, our faith grows. Remembering how God fulfilled His plans in the lives of Bible greats like Queen Esther and others reminds us of a crucial truth. Through Christ's finished work on the cross, we can do all He calls us to do. We can give our fears to God. We may not all be able to stand in the presence of royalty, but we can do the things we know God calls us to do. We can give full attention and effort to His call for our own individual lives. Like Esther, we, too, have been born for such a time as this.

JOURNAL THE ISSUES:

Meditate on Philippians 4:13: *"I can do all things through Christ which strengtheneth me."* (KJV)

How do *you* battle fear?

_____

_____

PRAYER:

Heavenly Father, I need Your help so much to overcome my fear of (name it). But you have told us not to be afraid. You have said You would strengthen us and help us. By the power of Your Spirit, I give You my anxiety and ask for Your strength to overcome my fear. In Jesus' name, I pray. Amen.

ENDNOTES

[1] John Foxe, *Foxe's Book of Martyrs, Updated and Abridged*, Barbour Publishing (2001).

[2] http://www.christianpost.com/article/20080409/bible-tops-america-s-10-favorite-books-of-all-time/index.html

[3] http://www.evanwiggs.com/revival/history/revfire.html

AUTHOR'S NOTE TO READERS

I hope you have been inspired, strengthened and encouraged by reading *Bible Miracles: 32 Daily Devotions and Journal to Inspire Today's Woman*. May the Lord continue to bless you.

For information regarding additional material (including additional copies or bulk supplies of this book and speaking engagements), please send a self-addressed envelope to:

Barbara Hemming
P.O. Box 84
Ashton, MD 20861

or

Contact the Author at:
hemmisur@yahoo.com